CASCADE OF ODES

John J. McKenna

iUniverse, Inc.
Bloomington

Cascade of Odes

iUniverse books may be ordered through booksellers or by contacting:

iUniverse
1663 Liberty Drive
Bloomington, IN 47403
www.iuniverse.com
1-800-Authors (1-800-288-4677)

ISBN: 978-1-4620-1107-0 (pbk)
ISBN: 978-1-4620-1108-7 (ebk)

Printed in the United States of America

iUniverse rev. date: 4/12/2011

INTRODUCTION

When I was a much younger man, my mind opening more and more to the ideas and practices of eastern philosophies, I often felt the desire to bring my father, a depression-era son of Irish immigrants, around to my way of thinking about the nature of life and the universe. I never succeeded. Sometimes in my own reading or mental wanderings I would happen across a concept which I felt sure would do the job, but later over dinner we'd end up arguing. He already knew the answers – or, at any rate, was compelled to posture as if he did – and he believed, apparently, that anger proved his authority on many subjects. Eventually I stopped trying to change him.

On the surface of things, you could say that I was esoteric and he was pragmatic. I was hippie-dippy. He was old school, and catholic school at that. He was a realist and I was a romantic.

Recently then, when he agreed to smoke some marijuana to combat the effects of cancer, that forgotten, young part of me grew hopeful. I haven't smoked pot for years, but it certainly had its place in the formation of my world view. Maybe Dad would experience a relaxing of mental constraints and spontaneously open to the ancient wisdom of his light body, or some shit. When, on the day of the adventure, after he'd begun smoking, he decided he simply HAD to have more music in his life – and would I move his stereo to his bedroom — I took it as a good sign. But, alas, the music was not rock 'n' roll. It was country. He didn't decide to grow his hair and take a four month retreat to an

1

ashram. No one who could listen to country western music while high would ever do that.

Recently I said something to my father which really touched him, which he said meant more to him than if he'd won the lottery. I've been a father myself for eight years now, and often when I'm interacting with my eldest daughter I feel the mantle of Fatherhood, as passed from my own father, draped over my shoulders. I know that I am to her what he was to me. I'm reminded, quite viscerally, of what he was to me. The thing that comes through, which was so comforting to me as a child, and which I am gratefully empowered to pass on, is a glowing abundance of warmth and tenderness and unconditional love. When I told my father this, tears filled his eyes.

Maybe when I was in my twenties I wanted to be closer to my dad, and questioned how that could be possible if we disagreed so fundamentally in our ontological views. Today I'm glad to know that none of that matters. The reason I even wanted more closeness with him had less to do with the thoughts in his mind and more to do with the love in his heart. And that is my father's most outstanding characteristic. The love in his heart beams out at you, makes you glad to be in his presence.

Of course our life's accomplishments prove what we really are. I'm aware of many details of my father's life. He received a lot of education. He had a career in education. He's a father six times over. He's a sports enthusiast who believes he *coulda ben somebody if not for that lousy bum leg!* (the same bum leg which endowed him with his ferocious drive as an athlete in the first place.) I guess he made a table once, which had three legs and wobbled. He regales anyone who will listen with ironic and hilarious stories of his rich, colorful and colorfully populated childhood.

To me, though, his most outstanding achievement is his second marriage. Those of us who know my father and my stepmother Annmarie know that they are absolutely crazy about each other, that for nearly thirty years now they've been thoroughly united, as in love as any two high school sweethearts, that they would be content to bask in each other's company for the rest of eternity. Such a harmonious union! Like the essence of yin and yang, masculine and feminine combining to create a wholeness that is complete unto itself, at the end of the day the life he has created with her amounts to the fulfillment of his purpose and of everything he ever desired. I think the poems in this book will bear that out.

That's why, on the day he tried marijuana, he didn't awaken to yoga or zen or chakras or chanting. He awakened, for maybe the ten thousandth time, to the love of his life. He called to her. She was nearby, as always. And as that country music song played, he held her in his arms and they danced: his favorite thing in the world.

He's such a romantic.

— John J. McKenna, Jr.

TRUE LOVE

Another anniversary
creeps lovingly in
to honor the bridge
of our joining
to pay tribute
to memorialize
this joyful crossing
while bursting through
ominous clouds of dread
and darkness

Then rending the clouds
leaking cracks of light
to heat our hands
in preparation for
relentless battle

Knowing that hearts
that truly love
will never dim
as true love
never diminishes

Illness

This Christmas
swept up on a totally
unprepared relic
consumed by thoughts
of the value of survival
with no room for visions
of sparkling candles shooing away darkness
fancy baubles, or thoughtful gifts
Yet, buried in the throes
of pending oblivion
there is a beacon of love
that shines brilliantly through
the shadowy, bottomless sadness
This is the powerful love
that wrapped two, true lovers
in warmth and care
for 28 years that is now
extending into this bleakest of times
to demonstrate its
strength and dedication
the heart-rending struggle
ensuing in these most difficult times
while this most loving duo
marches bravely across the battlefield
proudly waving a banner
highlighting sustaining hope
and hereafter fighting for lives of value

Settled Deep

a little girl
with darkened curl
tripped easily into my life

she nested there
with feelings rare
a complete and loving wife

the years slip quickly and warmly by
she settles deep within our bliss
eyes wide open
Her lips always pursed for early
passionate kiss

should we begin to reach
from our heaven there
or wander from the zestful day
to a peaceful bier

like each day through
how we dance and sing
we'll still do
in the going

Sought/Found

I sought a friend
I found one

I sought a lover
I found one

I sought a wife
I found one

I sought an equal
I found one

Then I sought
Harmony, peace, joy
I found all three

Now that I have
what I so feverishly sought,
fortunately found,

I'll surmount any obstacle
I'll swallow any disappointment
I'll ignore any hurt
I'll sacrifice willingly

To hold close, forever
this composite of full love
personified in,
emanating from,
my Annmarie

THINKING ABOUT

I think about
How constant you are
How rare when
Your bright ways
Aren't lighting up my life

I think about
How good it is
To have you tight by my side
Through somewhat busy times
Through busy-busy times
Especially through decadent times

I think about
How you are
with beauty, kindness, wisdom
Interlaced with
sustaining understanding

I think about
the crazy, twisted path
to your open door

I think about
How you touch me in
warm arms welcoming
the wild and risky stranger
with charming way

I think about
How your tamed me
and redirected me
To the basic, the good

I think about
How captive I am
within the soft, beautiful web
of our love

THE QUILT

The quilt of love
        is a many threaded covering

Some tenuous threads
        lightning hot

Some tenuous threads
        brittle and cold

Still the basic, enveloping fabric
        resists sporadic cold

By wrapping in steady, sustaining warmth
Smothering dissidence
        in a passion of caring, understanding,
        acceptance

Huddle under this miraculous mantle
Together, toasting its resilience

PINNACLE

To be loved fully
such a rare thing

To be loved completely
such a beautiful thing

Who on this pinnacle
would dare or care
to look down

consider dabbling
          on lower levels
attending to lesser concerns
Only the over-confident
only the foolish

Certainly not
          the wonderful person
          who loves me

Certainly not
          the not so wonderful person
          who loves her

FLOW

The tides of passionate love
rage in and ebb softly out

A sometimes rough
an always consistent flow

Who would want
a never turbulent, always
bland flow

Not I, whose passions run deep
Not you, whose passions run pure

Visage

What joy to see your relaxed face
in all its full beauty so clear
so easy to see. I must work
hard and diligently to keep the
face of the person I love relaxed.
To have the joy again and again
of seeing its uniqueness reflecting
on all surrounding and especially
intersecting deeply with me

SONG

Grow in strength and wisdom
my repenting, forgiving,
always loving ally

Grow in bending and bearing
with each and every storm
To stand alone when I
have failed away

Then I'll know
my songs are sung in
a better, more melodious way

My heart will revel in the singing
the song
accomplished

225

You can't help but admire
those folks who
when faced with a task
confront it straight on
with no question to ask
They just do what right now
has to be done
Delaying for time the
meaning of fun
Working it through to the
fruitful end
success the reward at
the last of the bend
When such a person glides
into your life
it's the pleasure of pleasures
when she's your loving wife
Spending her day shining rays
of exampling light
Piercing the gloom of
an overcast blight
Lifting with integral goodness
and love
a know-it-all person from
down to above

My Choice

The problem may be that
I love you too much
with expectations so demanding
they're frivolous and such

The problem may be my
dreaming of bright, airy heights
Too often resulting in
fruitless frights

The real task may be
myself to bevel
Thereby lowering the
fancied level

Then to mute the sweet
and the song
to forever fester in
knowing wrong

If it's a forced choice
that just has to be
Then I have no choice
but to choose you over me

HARBOR

Our little boat
weighted with its cargo of love
sailed through turbulent seas
weathered terrible storms
to finally land in a safe port
where we gleefully leaped ashore,
at a peaceful place
less harrow, less furrow
a place to rest, to heal
a time to see, to hear, to feel,
time completely together
time to be careful with time
filling open days, beckoning weeks
with the vitality of freedom
no reason to falter, no reason to slip
slowly inhale, exhale
pure fresh air
bathing in the warm rain
of hope realized, catch
the soft, white flakes of faith
on happy upturned faces
disciples strapped securely
in the harness of courage

Each day holding hands, holding hearts
living in full, living in love
before the sun sets, before
the dark clouds descend
before precious days dwindle away

PLACES

You lift me
> to hidden places
> to places I've never been
> to places of comfort, trust, joy
> passion, love.

I live now
> in these places
> so warm and so happy

Keep me forever here
in these places
wrapped in your arms
held in your heart

As I will forever keep you
in these places
wrapped in my arms
embedded in my heart

In Cold Morning Light

Sitting chill and still
        in cold morning light
looking across
        at a curled, sleeping form

Wondering where dreams go
        seeking what
        love lost
        love found

too awake to wait
        compulsively touch
        to awaken
        eyes opening
        words forming
        arms reaching

Being warmed now
        by the unfolding
        in the enfolding

to be surrounded and filled
        by the encompassing
to be loved again
        another day

One More Time

Talk with me one more time
Both carefully listening and hearing
Walk with me one more time
Holding hands, moving in soft rhythm

Dance with me one more time
Close together, smoothly gliding
within our harmony

Banter with me one more time
Exchanging warm, humorous
mollifying words

Steal away with me one more time
where we can shed the immediate world
to revel in our loving selves

Come home with me one more time
So two hearts can nestle together
in our haven

Love me one more time
In a place with no room
for defenses

Then love me all times
As I love you

GATHERING

I often ask myself
what did I ever do
To deserve the most special love
of the most special you

Oh, I've done some few good things
stumbling along the way
but they're far outnumbered
by the bad things
enacted day by day

Yet I've begun to gather together
deep within myself
led there by you
my beautiful, magic elf

I swear I'll keep improving
as long as you are by my side
As we cruise along so lovingly
On our unique and thrilling ride

Need

My eyes pursue the sight of you
My ears seek the sound of you
My nose inhales the scent of you
My hands crave the feel of you
My heart bleeds love for you
My being needs to wrap around you
Over and over and over

I love you
for the way you are
for what I am

for your giving
for what you make of me
for the mysterious pieces of me
you unmystify

for reaching into my heart
ignoring the bad
tugging out the good
into brightness
the good few others
bothered to find

Because you lead me
through the catacombs
of my life
to an open, warm, loving place
with lilt, laughter, song and dance

Because
you came
to make me better
despite my weakness
to make me complete

You have done all this
by being you
the foundation
upon which
I build my house
of true love

1/10/97 Make up

Mean roads appear
        unexpected, inescapable

Pace steadily, resolutely on
No dalliance

Another proving ground
For clear vision, high ideals

Where strong and good
Again lead the way

Knowing that with perseverance
Sure feet will soon strike
        smooth pavement

To be greeted with
        bright sun grinning
        from a blue sky

Then honor guarded
        along the way
By bending, gesturing
        kiss blowing flowers

Walk slowly, serenely appreciative
Linked in our calm stride
With confident love

Travel on
Dressed in joy
Renascent coupling
Fevered in contrast

ORNITHOLOGY

My oh so beautiful, loving bird
       must rest in our warm nest for a time
There I'll stroke her ruffled feathers so often
       she'll soon feel quite sublime

I'll fetch luscious berries
       For her tender little beak
To feed them ever so quietly
       week after patient week

I'll then fetch garlands of roses
       to drape 'round her neck
giving the only ways I know
to not become a ruined wreck

But soon enough her tiny feet
       will pulse and start to prance
Then we'll both be real eager
       for a wild Irish dance

I'll take one mighty leap
       onto her fluttery wings
then we'll soar high and free
       to throbbing music and wonderful things

LANGUAGE

The words I really mean
Are soft and warm

They rise from the depths
of my heart

Filtered carefully
Through the knowing me

Filled with the deepest love
that I possess

Those other words
the harsh and cold ones

Spill over from a dark pit
From another time, another place

Unwanted words
Unauthored by me words

They burn my tongue
They crush my soul

Banish them forever
To their malignant hole

You only deserve
My pure words of love

Simple, direct and true
with love to you

DREAM TO REALITY

Walk the road of dreams with intent and courage
Buoyed by self awareness

Walk the road with care and attention
Better to end the journey intact

Walk the road with grace and flair
Better to complete the journey light of heart

Walk the road with an openness to the
surrounding beauty
Sample these riches as you go

Walk the road with a discerning eye for hazards
Detour if you must for a little while only
to return to the road

Walk the road bravely, accepting the
occasional stub, stumble or fall

Realize such opportunity for renewing the spirit
regaining the pace

Walk the road knowing
I walk here beside you
loving till its end

FLOWERS FOR ANNMARIE

Whose tears lurk so close
To her smiling presence

Whose tender kindness
Encompasses so much of her being

Whose soft gentleness
Is a joy to behold

Whose love
Is my miracle

While I jostle her
My love intensifies

She's a rare jewel
I burnish in my strange ways

I grow
In her glow

CARDIAC SYMPATHY

My Annmarie is small and sensitive
With a big, encompassing heart

A heart that beats so fiercely
Next to mine

Some rare times its throbbing love
Skips a bit from the cold of mine

Even then it radiates such heat
It melts the frost away from mine

I then warm to its pulsating love
So deep within me it feels like mine

Back from the missing
I claim an eternal valentine

her heart is mine

Wings

Your gossamer wings brush against me
wrap around me, encircle me
with a hope, with a love, that
closes the deepest crannies in this
lonely, longing heart

They beat a soft, slow rhythm
through the hours of every day
carrying away each plaintive need
and every crying part

while flying me to a special place
I'd never thought to chart

As long as they keep beating
in their silky loving way, there
is nothing in this wide world
that could ever keep us apart

A River of Love

A river of love
flows ever so surely
through every inch of my heart
Beginning its journey
Seductively filling every crack, every crevice
right from the tumultuous start

This river's been flowing along now
for 16 and more years
And its soft steady movement
persistently insists
on washing away the tears, the fears

Oh sometimes it slows
under torrential rain
and stutters a bit on bumpy terrain
But it quickly returns
to a heart warming pace
and gracefully swallows implements of pain

Then continues its flowing
under a bright shining sun
Reminding two hearts
of all that's been won

Keep flowing and flowing
our river of love
To carry your burden
to the sweetness above

For without you
all that would be left in your wake
Would be dry sands of sorrow
where lost souls forsake

While Days are Sizzling

While days are sizzling
Under a hot, summer sun
While days are crisp
Under a waning, autumn sun
While days are bitterly cold
Under a retreating, winter sun
While days are promising
Under a renewing, spring sun

You hold me
Deep within a love
for all seasons
A lover of trust, truth, beauty
and fire

A love that weathers
     the wildest storms
     the bullying wind
     the pounding rain
     the raging tide
     the blinding snow
     the hottest, most searing sun

A love that catches and holds close
     the gentle day
     the warm breeze
     the quiet rain
     the lapping wave
     the gentle snow flake
     the softest, most soothing sun

A sheltering yet elevating love
Protecting while leading
to better thoughts, better ways,
better times and
to a better me

Following

Who is first to leave this place
Who is left to trudge this road alone
      will drink in thirst from the well of memory
      to taste the joy still known

Who is first to leave this place
Who is left to struggle along
      will touch each spot
      that both have touched
      to hear a voice
      to see a smile
      through darkness lit by still known

Who is first to leave this place
Who remains with broken heart
      will rally through the terrible pain
      to move in faith
      to move in hope
      in belief still known

Who is first to leave this place
Who is to steadfast battle on
      this deadening, bitter path
      will hold head high
      to realize that quite so very soon
      the time to follow
      to reach, to touch, to hold
      the first to leave this place
      will happen in a newer place
      again their very own
      this too is still known

Apology

To tell you all those things
I am sorry for, to tell
you I never love enough
to tell you of my shame
never spoken, of not doing

In what tone, in what
whisper, bending, kneeling
not so rigid, on what
I might have been, don't
seem to be, begging strength
to admit weakness

I must confess, lean close
for you to hear, words for you
my breath washing across
your cheeks

You will answer, as you do,
nudge me to a safer way
absent rant absent rave
absent scathing, to your love
that always sees, that always listens
that always waits, there, for me

STORMS

Storms unexpectedly descend
       for the strong to weather
       to appreciate the bright sun more fully

For who is to say
       life is always a blissful journey

What's to enjoy in sameness
       over and over

Let the good battle the bad
       hand to hand
       within the rules of the game
       then to win in fairness, dignity
       to be crowned with joy
       for the championship of love

Rancor

You dance so easily, so beautifully
      through our life
      stretching, twisting, reaching, twinkling
      with care, with love, with sparkle

When suddenly, one dark moment
      a terrifying cloud descends, envelops

You hesitate, you flutter
      You screech to a broken halt
      losing grace, losing charm, losing love
      while oozing anger, rancor
      and even hate

Where does this unexpected, unseasonably
      dark, crazy lapse come from
      the outside
      the inside

I want to know

We can't possibly want or need
      this fast moving terror
      to darken, to block out
      the sunshine of our love

Let us then
      rend the cloud
      vanquish the darkness
      swallow and spit out
      the terror
      allow the wild canaries
      to sing
      forever

A Little Valentine's Day Poem

Though it's Valentine's Day
I love and speak the same

My heart is all days filled
Since the time you called my name

Now what to do
With cupid's frenzy about

I'll kick my heels
And emit a happy shout

But silly show
Is a game I rarely play

So I'll grip your hand
And again I'll softly say

You've brought a joy
I never really had

So good I feel guilty sometimes
And act a little bad

But always know
And never shed a tear

That my love for you
Shall forever be deep in here

To Live

Walk the sands of the Bay
Emit the fragrance of a smoked pipe
Caress the head of the best, canine pal
Read a deep book in depth
Hold the warm hands of little ones
Touch the needs of the lost
Hold tight those loved and loving
Match the love of the most loved
Toast all good
Denounce all bad
Live to live

THE DOER AND THE DREAMER

I am plodding patience
spontaneously erupting
in flames of anger
easily doused by silent guilt

the dreamer of unrealizable dreams
the ponderer of the meaningless
the promiser of the unpromiseable
the deep thinker of the thinkless
the absent overseer of the real workers

However
        I am not a denier
        of who I am: the one
        who loves you

You are the walker not the talker
the bread and the knife
the crystal goblet and the wine
the hot hug in a cold bed
the warm fire heating our home
the conscience balancing our life
the doer of things to be done
the bright smile breaking through dark clouds
the designer decorating the drab
the lover of the unloveable
the cutter through to the heart of things
the best of persons
my life, and
thankfully
my wife

DASH

a silver Buick glides easily
into a parking area, two figures
shadowed by a golden beauty,
gingerly approach a starting line
they hunker down, prepare for
a stretch run, looking around
to see the few spectators
dwindling away, mounds of material
things, fading sunlight reflecting off
a litter of jugs, dusty trophies
a billboard displaying snapshots
of giving tarnished by obligation, of
deserted dance floors, of barren
relaxation places, looking forward
to see a beckoning tape, they
take drinks from a bottle labeled spiritual
feel a bubbling then a boiling within
they leap away with confidence
and power, certain success
surely breaking a tape, then
as winners wrapped warmly
in a flag of love

Mission Accomplished

Climb a hill
      never a mountain
Claw, scratch to surmount
      times loving, times lusting
Crawl forward
      exhausted, frustrated
Slip backward
      land on a rock
Surprised at the solidity here
      of fulfillment, peace, love
Why continue the climb
      mission sought
      mission accomplished

THE GOODNESS OF THIS WOMAN

the goodness of this woman
lights a fire in my heart
the dregs of doom that live there
burn off to brightness out of dark

It soars around my person
blasts open the chambers of this heart
to let fresh faith in
despair to slip out

The goodness of this woman
washes the film from these blind eyes
to refix with clear vision
as if I'm born again

Sinners entangled in sin's vast net
feel a slackening in the web
when they sense the goodness of this woman
and begin to hope again

It glides across waters
that sharply divide
and joins in peace the hostile shores
to easily receive the bickering tides

The goodness of this woman
brings highs where there were lows
smothering the terrible sound, the terrible sight
of real and imagined woes

The goodness of this woman
brings a love I've never known
so I kneel each day
I pray, I pray
it will encase me
'til time exists no more

WITNESS

My body still tends to labor
in the desert of the past
in the sadness of sins never forgiven
of that never said, never done
always in fear of years closing around
with terrible darkness

My heart then carols
enough of this self-pity
pumping me into movement
through a sleeping home
through rooms whose beauty
is cheerily reflected
off a myriad of bright mirrors
to windows that witness
a glowing moon whose reaching rays
shine happily down
on the pulsating waters of the Bay

My mind joins the move
to contemplate a family
whatever their differences
that deeply care
a life, whatever the duration
that allows a freedom to do
each day

My soul then connects
bringing the beguiling breath
of sustaining life
to this growing movement

We all rally up a majestic stairway
to enter a room of rich color
and see a petite form
curled up on a large bed
the soft music of her slumber
fills the room
my feet being to shuffle in rhythm
my heart thumps with joy
my mind waves a baton of respect
my soul nods in appreciation
for we all know
here sleeps the queen of good
the real joy of Christmas
the only gift worthy of Christmas
for this and much more
we love her

ISLAND

Deep within interwoven hearts
rests our secret island, a serene spot,
nestling on soft, white sands,
surrounded by calm, warm waters,
under a clear, blue sky dotted by
lazily drifting clouds

It is to this private place we run
when the weather is hostile, the talk
tends to bruise, the walk is late arriving,
helping seemingly hapless, the jug
of joy leaking

It is here we hide and bide,
touch more tenderly, talk more freely,
amble more caringly, hug more lovingly,
shed the shackles of constriction

It is here we are reborn, renewed,
reinvigorated, a renaissance pair
It is here we are readied
to return out there, clearer
of mind, stronger of body,
longer of stretch, more welcome
to toil, more accepting of strife,
purposeful

We leave our private, precious island,
more in love than ever,
buoyantly riding the crest
of our surging wave of years,
together, forever

EXPECTATION

The years to come will prance in joyfully:
time here, time there, we will sit
at our table, as we taste fine food,
sip red wine, delve passion, compassion,
warmed by soothing fire, eyes locked,
so much ours, within each time,
reborn, restored, after which,
we will dance, in step, in harmony
to our sweet music, the music
we chose, we cherish, we love

ODYSSEY

In a state of turmoil
tottering on the deck of indecision
he clambered aboard a boat
bound on a mysterious voyage

He huddled in a small, creaky cabin
as the boat limped and waddled away

Suddenly the sea became wild and angry
lashing the boat with vicious waves
rocking it madly back and forth

He was roughly thrown
to the cabin floor
crazed, confused, fearful

Magically the vessel righted
to begin a skillful passage
around shoals, beyond groundings
assuming full throttle upstream

It continued to sail carefully along
to finally anchor in a peaceful stream
where he slipped bravely overboard
into smiling, beckoning water
which carried him supportively forward
within soft, gently swelling waves,
into bright sunshine
then washing him up on destiny's island
to listen to seashells whispering
sweetness in his ear
while a chorus of pelicans sing in harmony
of caring, of loyalty

to rest on his weariness
over serene sands of compassion
to swing joyfully in a hammock of happiness
then to sleep soundly
wrapped in the warm blanket
of true love

WITHIN LOVE

As wild as the wind
that blows winsomely
over land, over sea
for purpose known, unknown
or the falling snowflake
that drifts from the sky
through time
to sodden earth

So my heart
resisting isolation
whatever the elements
searches the darkness
for you
Where I can rest
in your accepting mind
in your willing will

There faith fastens in hope
for the best to come
with you
with me
within love

The Whisper

For years duped by time, as ally, as friend,
sudden crush under reality, see time,
as mortal enemy, as nemesis, sibilantly whispering,
hissing, you age

Rage against age, rage against whisper, the whisper
whispers
again, you see less
you hear less, you move less, you are less

scream at the whisper, no wrinkles, no fat,
no bulge, lean, hard, squeeze my hand,
if you can, speak up you almost mute,
take me on fairly

The whisper whispers on, what have you
Accomplished, lately, without smoke, without
mirrors,
who have you loved, lately, without restriction,
what are you, lately, a carcass, emitting
stench of could-be's, should-be's, would-be's

Gather wits, deride the whisper, does a whisper
know what I know, having solved the mystery
of happiness, having formed a partnership, with
loved, loving partner, collected evidence,
followed clues, identified, caught,
annihilated culprits, slayed dragons of despair

Then to reach, to touch, to live in nirvana,
especially on this day, milestone, February 9, 1999,
partners still, more loving, more loved,
actively resting, blissfully, in haven, in home,

canopied by the bluest sky, anchored
to ebbing, flowing water, surrounded
by lush greenery, as night descends,
bathing in the soft light of the dogstar,
safe from the grasping tentacles
of time, immune to dark whispering,
free to rejoice, free to celebrate
internalization, externalization,
by and in love

Darkness and Light

It seems this day
I don't know who I am
I sleep, dream, toss, wake
to confusion, despair
I think of all I have not seen
of all I will never see
The sleep, dream, toss, wake
are enshrouded in darkness
My thirst for movement, onward, upward
has always been, never slaked,
did it run away

I now know if I lived for all time
all things I would do
could never be done

I was once a little boy limping
despising the limp
yet thinking I would live forever
time to cure self, others

Another day, another page
beginning darkness
ensuing in darkness
enduring in darkness

Peering into this terrible darkness
I glimpse a halo of light
surrounding a shapely silhouette
dancing to me
leaping into my arms
holding me with passion

taking my hand
leading me through dispelled darkness
into the brightness of love

THE RUNNING

Walking in fog, in mist
into each other's lives
more than 14 years ago
Stepping slowly at the start
then faster, then hesitating, then faster again
Breaking into a run
in tandem, into clearer air
running through good times, bad times
still in tandem
As the path stretched farther, farther
holding closer, closer
stride matching stride
bodies straining alongside
Leaping over obstacles
on a sometimes difficult way
laughing in the happiness
crying in the sadness
Striving harder
when the terrain's resistant
to the steady beat of running feet
Path becomes easier in the running
despite menacing time running beside
the highest hills dwarf
the biggest problems shrink
Running on almost level ground
relishing the easy running
seeing, smelling the flowers
Still the thorns
reaching, scratching from those deceivingly beautiful
roses
stinging deeply in the passing
Rest for a bit
inspect the hurt

remove the prickles
allow no fester
Rising, run again
forward, never looking back
run in hope, run in faith
whatever the pace of time
whatever the bumps
whatever the stress

Run on, and on, and on
no finish line
no end
enveloped in the best love

MILESTONE

Another milestone
In our journey

How far have we travelled
A loving way

How long has it been
Seems like always

How good has it been
Seems like perfect

When did it start
Seems like first sight

When will it end
Seems like never

Why so pleasurable
It's lovingly ours

What to do
Stride easily forward

Stay on the path
Avoid brambles

Hand in hand
Step in step

Exude in the warmth
Drink in the view

Follow the light
Together forever

My Harbor

Beating waves of despair
Pound against me

Incessant beat
Breath sucking beat

Gulping, gasping
Blindly groping

Fingers madly reaching
Finding tangled mass
familiar hair

Hands frantic cupping
Etched contours
            familiar face

Waves subsiding
Breathing resuming

Arms enfolding
Love harboring

THE ANSWER

Love or convenience
What is your name

Or strangest of strange
Perhaps you're the same

While we weep and we keen
Over burgeoning hearts

The need to self serve
Forever restarts

Do we need one another
As part of a game

Is the march along love
Always the same

Can it be possible
To give and cavort

Or is it always predestined
To callously abort

I give you the answer
My curious friend

Believe it or not
I've turned that bend

The answer is simple
As you'll hopefully see

I trust her
She trusts me

PETULANCE

Little boy arrayed like man
Stamps his foot in pique

Stroke his glistening brow
Wrap him in love

Grow him up again
Back where he belongs

Too Busy

I look at people
I used to know

I know now
I never knew

How could I
Too busy knowing me

How could they
Too busy knowing them

Not so self-involved anymore
There's time to know

I and they
Passing in the past

You the present
You the future

I'm busy knowing you now
Hope you're busy knowing me

Watching Over

I see her sleeping
That curled up little form

I pray her dreams aren't fitful
I hope they're soft and warm

She's tired from fretting
About things big and small

Stretching, waking now
Like an unfurling ball

Big eyes open
Race the space to mine

Embracing looks
Banter first, then shine

Dream's storm
Abates in the reflection

Another precious piece
Joins my collection

Doctor's Visit

My heart went to the doctor today
Captive within her

I waited for their return
Waited and worried

Nothing could be wrong
Or could it

Life would stop
With a despairing wail

Fullness to emptiness
Such a short ride

To reach and grasp
To slip so quickly away

It can't be
It won't be

My heart will safely return
Still captive

Our Fire

We sit by the fire
Soaking up the warmth

Peering into the flames
Seeking, seeing mysteries

Mysteries of life and love
Mysteries of hopes and dreams

Catalyst fire
Tap wells within

Heat what we know
Simmer soft and slow

Lick around and temper
Our bond of love, you know

Burn away the weak
Soar around the strong

Hold in your fiery arms
Scorch away the wrong

You are
as close as my skin
warmed by your fire
shielded by your strength
caressed by your kindness

the light
cleansing my eyes
brightening darkness
leading me to a better way

the window through which
the sun shines
the moon beams
the stars twinkle

the form, the substance
reaching into every corner
of my heart

the talented Director
who raises the curtain
on life's stage
about an astounding
twenty and more years
with you as the star
I as the supporting player

that is why
I loved you then
I love you now
I will love you forever
'til the curtain falls
Then I will continue to love you
in the hereafter

Another milestone
Another landmark
Another special day
not so unlike all our days
each special in its own way
on our landscape of togetherness
most days warm waters wash over
some days stormy clouds hover
few days violent winds buffet

Through all days
            whatever the portent
            we blissfully cavort
            on a stage
            built solid
            on a foundation of love

A love that weathers
            any storm

A love fittingly costumed
            in a garland
            of faith, trust and hope

A love that continues
            to grow
            to expand
            to encompass
            all the coming days
            within the invincible bond
            of two welded, melded hearts

GOLDEN STRAND

There is this golden strand
we hold, we follow
as it threads its way
among things that change
while never changing

Some may wonder
where we follow to

It's hard to explain
It may be hard
for others to see
what we know
what we feel

Holding, following
our golden strand
we are never lost

Bad things happen
people hurt, suffer
get old, die
time unfolds
curtains fall

Yet we will not, cannot
ever let go
ever stop following
our golden strand
that binds us
so fast in our love
a love
that molds us

as we lovingly unravel
the mysteries
of each other

FIDES QUAERENS INTELLECTUM

Another Christmas
galloping faster than before
dancing, prancing on the village square
colorful banners streaming
hoofs glistening in the light

Yet a persistent cloud still hovers
darkening, intensifying
emitting swelling, withering impact
on the senses
gradually dimming clarity
feeding growing, clammy fear

Slowing if not stemming this malignant growth
is faith on a quest to know

Smothering this angst
is knowing your rallying love
surrounds and fulfills me

MARVELOUS CREATION

So glad you were born
To Lucy and Frank

Such a generous gesture
I have them to thank

To think if they hadn't
Where would I be

So lonely and dejected
With nothing to see

By their thoughtful conception
They gave me a life

That's uplifted and soaring
Without any strife

I must always remember
To give them just due

For without such pairing
I'd never have you

So on this day of your birth
I look with devotion on that pair

Who produce for my love
The sweetest, most fair

Each day I ponder
Their marvelous creation
As I revel and bask
In our loving relation

JEWEL

Place your loving, precious heart
deep within my strong and caring hands
to be gently protected
till the end of trickling sands

this unique, rare jewel I always sought
but never could buy
made me so sad throughout the years
I could naught but cry

But now it's here
to caress and watch in awe
the most beautiful I've ever seen
or even ever saw

I'll kiss it in the morning, all day
and throughout the night
while loving the sheen radiance
with all my meager might

OUR LOVE

It waits patiently in the dark
to rise alert with the early sun
to spread warmth throughout our home
to every niche, to every crevice
supporting the very structure
with subtle strength

It gently moves into our hearts
washing away any pang
smoothing over any sharpness
healing any hurt
easily surviving
any rare moment of neglect

It is a unique giving
each to the other
indissoluble giving
indestructible giving
with a power to even transcend
the chasm of death
In its special way it provides
It is the magical immunity
which protects us from any betrayal
of one to the other
And if you listen carefully enough
you may hear its soft melodious purr
whisper our love's reassurance
in this poem

CLOCKWISE

Tick, tick, ticking away
      the time clock that never stops
Ticking fast in years
      of scattered sowing
      bouncing on unyielding soil
Ticking not so fast in years
      of desperate reaping
allowing moments to cull the reward crop

Ticking through bad times
      drought drying dreams
      blight besieging loneliness
      storms washing away hope

Ticking through better times
      leavened by soft rains of kindness
guided by gentle winds of understanding
buoyed by the spirit of love

Ticking now at a scramble to resting
another milestone
another chance to leap and
reawaken, expunge, to
be reborn
to burn the decrepit
sagging barn, overstuffed
with bleak memories
debilitating misgivings
deadened paths, paths
never taken

Leap on the chance
dance in cadence
with the ticking
around the roaring fire
wash in cleansing flames
revel in brightness
               away from shadow darkness

dance on, unfettered
               over dying embers
                    spilling ashes
                    ghosts dispelled
                    devils exorcised

               to our harm-tight silo
to store our magical crop
to preserve our harvest of love

Knowing we can, unblinking,
stare down the eyes of death
for if death is the end of love
we shall never die

1990

Irish bogs never seen
Craggy mountains never climbed

Wild dances never danced
Lilting songs never sung

Mighty races never run
Great achievements never achieved

Full caring never shared
Deep kindness never given

Until the mysterious delivery
of the complete gift
The embodiment of all ever sought
The end of a frantic search

Love worth dying for
Love worth living for

1991

Blink on you speckled Christmas light
Shatter night's darkness with your flight

Fall slowly little wrinkled snow
Soften edges where you go

Walk ever faster feverish feet
As hungry fingers grasp to treat

Descend O Yule this time of year
Dampen any hope of cheer

Mantle me in sorrow's shroud
So tight to smother all that's loud

Sink me in this dark abyss
There's nothing here for me to miss

Till you, a tiny candle light
To brighten up this lonely night

It's only then I start to stir
Love's awakening, a kind of myrrh

Lead me up with warming kiss
Lift me with your gentle bliss

Wrap me in your quilt of love
Then we lift our eyes above

1992

Take me gently on this new adventure
My feet dragging, my heart singing

Take me to a sweeping, sweeter view
My voice grumbling, my eyes shining

Take me to yet another realized dream
My steps stuttering, my soul stretching

Give me your soft, strong hand
Lead me, a fearful, expectant child

Into changing, brightening days
Guided by the shine of your persuasive love

Move me with your quiet rhythm
Blend our sway with easy grace

Dance as one in our new direction
Twirl away - just for a moment - then
        rush eagerly back into sheltering arms

A brief touch of cold
The reassuring warmth of your swift return

Pierce my dark brooding with your sparkle
Lessen my imagined burden
        with your upbeat cadence

Coax, cajole, and cater me
It's what I tease for

Waltz me through our new home
Waltz me to the beat and swell
    of our love

1993

Settled in our haven now
With comfort, hearth, and song

Strobed by a light that brightens
      each piece of space
Leading through the intimacy of love's ecstasy
      without constraint

Hearts beat in soft rhythm
      with the ebb and flow of the Bay

Minds rise with the glorious sun
      shining and sharing

Touching together things we never touched
Heated by a new dimension of glow

Finding here
      what was never there

A milieu of promise
A milieu of ever expanding selves

Breathing in slowly, deeply
Exhaling life's entanglements

Carefully holding the fruits of love
Expunging corners of darkness

Helping up our first Christmas tree here
      with an inner burst of passion
Decorating with candles of hope
Surrounding with gifts for love's extension

Breaking bread
      with those who share the source
      of ever burgeoning awareness

Dancing on our anvil of love
Watching the sparks fly
      wildly around us
As we are enveloped and tempered
      in our hearts' fire

1994

Christmas again bustling in, swirling carelessly
Not so breathless now
         this time around

A time reflecting sorrow's ache, deep loss
Magic sweetness never to be tasted again

A time reflecting disrupted union
Union thought to be perfect, lasting

Looking askance into winking, little lights
Bitter, baneful, transitory

Looking with annoyance
         on a lazily twirling, waving santa
         across the way
Bristling defiantly
         at baubles, dread, doom

Gloomily consorting
         with sickness, with death

Cards dwindling to a meaningless few
         not so glad tidings

Yet
         witness little boys growing gradually
                  into stalwart manhood
         witness linked adults steadily gaining
                  on that elusive grail, achievement
         witness the constant Bay
                  still coming, still going, still edifying
         witness the cavorting of a little, golden puppy
                  open, free to love, to be loved

especially witness my wife
>for all seasons, all reasons
>holding tight to love, to me
>over all trails, smooth, uneven, or rough
>never letting up, never letting go

Ergo
Toast the good, the beautiful
>drown the bad
>raise glass, heart, dreams

Sip slowly, tenderly the joie de vivre
>precious nectar
>constituted from real friends, bonded family
>harmoniously blended
>by the headiest of loves
>of this man for this woman for this man

1995

How fortunate
       to rejoice on another Christmas milestone
              with intertwining roots
              burrowing deeper
              extending further
              growing sturdier

How fortunate
       to each day see
              the tensile strength of offspring shoots

How fortunate
       to each day see
              the overwhelming beauty
                 of blooming flowers

Nothing can thwart, divert
       the expansion
       the solidification

Nothing can thwart, divert
       the intense delight

Neither storms
       nor dry spells
Neither pestilence
       nor weeds

A gardening adventure
       resulting in awesome success

Is there a magic wand wielded here
Is there a magic spell hovering over

Or is it a joy that inspires
a joy emanating from working, playing, sweating,
laughing
       in a garden of rich love

Thrusting hands together
       deep within yielding soil
       brushing shoulders
       brushing hearts

Laboring with a verve
       converting labor to bliss

Is there a mystery here
If there is a mystery
       the mystery is an unbelievable fortune
       allowing a meeting
          a teaching
          a loving so complete

I clasp greedily this good fortune
       a fortune nonexistent
       without the consummate loved, loving

1996

Waning in the good life
I walk on the wet, sleeping grass
  of my land
  thinking, *not so green anymore*

I look up at a leaden, weeping sky
  thinking, *how sad it seems*

My steps, like the years
  disappear as I walk
My dreams, like my steps
  wash away without trace

I'm in no hurry
  subsisting on gloomy plodding
  muttering, meandering
  hunched under the cloud
   called holiday season
  portending fleeting gifts, bitter garnish,
    hollow gusto

Remembering
  how friends, over time, come, go
  how mother, father, sisters, son
  slip through fingers to where

Remembering
  how offspring venture afar
  where head and heart lead

I rest for a moment
  on weathered, restraining logs
  only to feel a wet nose nuzzling

a warm tongue licking

my spirit skips a beat

I look to the house
        with its brightly lit
        many windowed charm
        my spirit skips another beat

I can now see
        a petite, dark-haired beauty
        bustling happily within

        my spirit begins to shed
        the rags of despair
        slip into the robe of love
        pulsate in the warmth

I jump to my feet
        to quicken steps
        to lengthen stride
        to enter home
        to gather and hold
        my forever Christmas

1997

Christmas days strung endlessly together
People strung mindlessly together
Words strung wordlessly together

Good times struggling with bad times
Good times whimpering away

Endless coming to an end
Mindless minding nothingness
Wordless crushed under its own weightlessness

Where to run for solace
Where to hide for rest
Where to find peace

Retreat within
> look to self
> extract order from disorder
> open the trap of trappings
> unsettle scores
> spit out disappointment
> see objectivity

Re-enter replenished
> take love in your arms
> dance majestically around the tree
> dance blithely over the gifts
> dance easily through the frills
> hold close, hold true

> > dance as one
> > > to the loved
> > > join hands

all dance together, in harmony, in rhythmic
balance
　　　surrounded by the strains of caring, giving
　　　merge hearts in a circle of merriment
　　　led by a baton of joy
　　　held in the hands of a conductor of love
　　　into a better, brighter time
Anniversary Time

time
to ponder/freshen past
to appreciate/savor now
to envision/pursue future
in our context
of love
love that can never rest
love that can never stop
love that can never die
February 9, 1986

The day
we declared
our love
to our world
knowing
we had
already declared
our love
to each other
As we ponder/freshen
As we appreciate/savor
As we envision/pursue

I offer
some few thoughts
from my heart
to your heart

TOAST

Night gathers softly around our home
cloaking in warming darkness
lights start to twinkle
across a brooding bay
the moon begins its graceful rise
in a darkening sky
within brightly lit windows is gentle bustle
supper's busy preparation surrounded by teasing
aroma
logs carefully arranged in a somber fireplace
then roaring to life on ignition
slender, pink candles are lit, to shine happily
on the reflecting glass of the table top

the anniversary scene is set
we sit to break bread, breathe milieu
toast love, hold hands, fast and forever

You

when I hear you, sweet tones magnify
when I hear you, ears attend
with ardor and applaud the gentle harmony;
when I hear you the soft music
easily washes away the harsh, the discordant

when I see you, pulse quickens
when I see you, eyes brighten
with joy and dance a dance
of caring; when I see you, beautiful visions
race wildly to encircle and imprison my heart

when you hold me, sinews strain
when you hold me, muscles harden
with delight and sing a song of pleasure;
when you hold me, warmth
swirls in eddies of passion
exhilarating, engulfing

As I love you, heart expands
As I love you, soul extends
with intensifying zeal to encompass
the best of living; as I love you
faith, fullness, fervor inextricably lock
to run interference through
all our years

Princess

A beautiful princess dances wildly,
seductively in a vineyard of brambles.
She easily brushes away the pricks
of thoughtless shrubs. She smiles her way
through the entanglements of smothering vines.
She caresses carefully the smallest of grapes.
A shy tear appears now and then
only to be quickly dried by warm and loving eyes.

Who are you, beautiful princess
so easily able to see good in bad.
Are you imprisoned by faith in what
you love or are you free, so free, you
can skip sprightly over the dark and the bad
to touch the light and the good. Is it
because you look up not down, you love
with such fervor?
Whatever the separation, the combination,
dance on sweet princess, while I watch
in awe, awe at the vigor, awe
at the constancy, while I passionately
feel the intensity of love for the
beautiful princess reaching to and
mating with her ardor

CHALLENGE

I bleed and I cry as I watch
our glorious years together
steam away far too fast

I strive mightily, yet vainly
to hold them
to plead with them to last

Why is it that years so precious
unlike years that betray your heart
can't rest for the time we're together
never really apart

It's the way of life I gather
the best years must flee to the sky
then float in their lofty position
to languish, and to laugh in the soft clouds so high

our option then my beloved
is to really quicken our pace
we can run wildly, pushed by tumultuous wind
pushed to be ever so swift

We shall run to match the speed
of the reckless years
holding our banner of love so high
we can proudly display, for all to see, our surely
greatest gift
We can cross the finish line of this race
with prancing, with power, draped in such grace
that the adversarial years will quickly smile down
just like a long lost friend
we will smile warmly back

heightened by knowing
we ran our very best, inseparably loving
from exciting beginning to satisfying end

MOUNTAIN

Caught in a silky web woven by love
we witness beautiful year flowering
upon beautiful year, each year seeking
a higher level up the side of a steep
mountain, a mountain of pleasure, of joy

We climb our mountain steadily, close,
lightening packs of unnecessaries, jettisoning
excess, shedding anxiety, fear, worry as
we go.

Climbing, the air becomes more pure
little slips, few stumbles, bring added agility.
Hand over hand, grasping each jutting, heart
over heart, gripping each outcropping;
Bumps, bruises stroked away by
caring ways, careless slippage made
up by buoyant spirits.

Stopping to rest at times, blithely casting
off packs, romping gaily, playing with abandon.

Simply interlocked, strong, supple we resume
onward, upward, renewed in zeal, the
valley below an indistinguishable blue.

A peak, a destination, difficult to see, to imagine,
clouded by the exhilaration, the ecstasy
of climbing together, such a blissful
climb neither needs nor wants a scaling.

We climb, climb ever higher, day by day,
inch by inch, year by year, mile by mile,

until our breath fails, until our strength
gives way, until we can climb no more,
to then wrap our souls in special wings,
to soar gracefully over our miraculous
mountain, still together, still intact,
still in love, basking in our fulfillment,
united forever, leaving behind a legacy
to love.

Mission

I discovered a rare and radiant flower
In a bleak and barren garden

I marveled at its brightness, its beauty
From a wary, careful distance

Then, one day, I ventured closer
The flower was even more beautiful
Beside me

Each day I would sit there
Watching, holding my breath
Feeling such tenderness

Till finally I gingerly stroked the flower
Whose warmth filled my hand, my heart

It now seemed to be my own
My very special flower

A ritual was born
A ritual of protecting my surprising prize
From encroaching weeds
Which would entangle, strangle

Gently patting
To soften surrounding soil

Softly watering deep roots
To provide necessary nourishment

My flower bloomed and blossomed

Becoming more beautiful
By the watch

Till one day
As I moved to ritual
Sly, vicious minds caught me
Shoved me away

Bewildered, buffeted
I was moved in a different direction
Away from my cherished prize

As the winds receded
I looked back
My flower's stem was badly bent
Her head was hanging, forlornly, dejectedly

Weeds were rapidly encircling
to close in
to strangle

the not-so-nestling soil
Was brittle, dry
I turned back
Racing with pounding heart
Trembling knees
To my beleaguered beauty

Kneeling, I carefully adjusted her graceful stem
Gently lifted her proud head

Re-arranged, re-adjusted, re-moistened
the shifting soil

Re-filled with ardor
Re-armed by once-in-a-lifetime love

I knew that no force, condition, nor obstacle
Could ever again
Deter, detour, or deny me

My direct and chosen mission
of prizing, caring, protecting
My most unique, cherished love

PERCEPTION

I fit briefcase and things into her car,
fussing about punctuality, the garage door
glides magically open, the car crookedly
descends the driveway, hands wave,
kisses blown, the car becomes smaller,
smaller, exit for the day, garage door glides
magically closed.
I enter the now silenced house, peaceful
quiet envelops, time to contemplate,
too soon I'm aroused by a ringing phone,
she arrived safely, if not on time, at school,
exchange of verbal correctness, exit contact for day.

I slide back into solitude, introspection,
deeper, deeper, darker, darker, till I reach
restless uneasiness, empty ache, gulping
for assistance I seek, reach for support,
find none from an empty house. I listen
for familiar sounds, quick tapping of dancing feet,
melody in a warm voice, loving beat
in her presence. I look for reassuring
sights, openness of reaching arms, sparkle
in loving eyes, seductive curve of giving lips,
only echoes, only mirages.

What price peaceful quiet, too steep, I stalk
the house, worry the clock, search the windows,
need, want, miss, long, peaceful quiet merges
into loneliness, impatient yearning feverish,
I hear her car return, garage
door glides magically open again, time
for re-entry, start to race to door,
catch myself, bridle the unbridled, assume

nonchalance, thinking how incredible, how nice,
more than twelve years, still need, want
her by side, more than ever, forever.

REALIZATION

In a moment or two
we will be married for too few, too fast years
Each of these years
        has slipped too quickly
        but so warmly by
With each year
        glittering more brightly
        than the last
So brightly at times
        I must shield my eyes
        to appreciate the beauty

I had never envisioned a life
        of such brightness and joy
I had never envisioned
        such stylish bending, blending
        of strong individuality
I had never envisioned
        a partner of such goodness

With these years
        as harbingers
        I reach in excitement and love
        to embrace the future

As I always reach
        in excitement and love
        to embrace
        the most giving
        the most loving
        of wives

ANNMARIE

How many times
have I said happy birthday

How many times
have I said I love you

My mind muddles
at the number
as passing time makes me wonder
why each time
makes my heart beat faster

MARCH 24, _____

Born this day
a long, short time ago
Bubbling, giggling, growing
in this time
Sharing good times
some bad times
Never wavering
Never judging
There when needed
with heart, with hand
There when wanted
with hug, with smile

Enjoying interests
Enduring hurts
Less caring for self
More caring for others

So much given
Too little gotten
Filled with a strength
an irrepressible kind
Filled with a love
that spills over

May this day
surround you in joy
May this joy
also spill over

To all your thoughts
To all your days

BORN

A day was born
Like no other

A person then
Like no other

Why the day
The way of things

Why the person
Someone was waiting

The day passes
The person lingers

Growing, laughing, crying.
Living, longing, looking

Here and there
Bits and pieces

Take a chance
Just a taste

Sometimes bitter
Most times bland

Another day
Another taste

Tart but sweet
Senses tingling

Sating time
Wait no more

CONTACT

I watched a dark haired beauty
Dance and prance over a parking lot

She was surrounded by an aura
An aura of spirit and mission
She was so vital, so real
Yet I dismissed her as unreal

Later I contacted with her
She was real, even more captivating
than I could have imagined

I was caught up beyond her beauty
with a directness softly leavened by sweetness
I was caught up with her easy lack of pretense
I was caught up with her warm and knowing way

Contact gradually increased in frequency
Contact gradually increased in intensity
Contact, not so gradually, escalated to beginning love

I had unexpectedly discovered what I despaired of
ever discovering
A complete, beautiful, loving person
A person to cherish and to be cherished by

Through a forest of entanglement
I pursued her
Through a forest of entanglement
I courted her
Through a forest of entanglement
We melded

The beginning, love burgeoned,
bloomed, blossomed
The serendipitous discovery
leading from despair to victory
A victory like no other

Now I carefully and tenderly hold
My invaluable prize
This still dancing, still sweet beauty
who bravely accompanied me though the thicket of a
lesser forest
This still non-pretentious beauty
Who settled so neatly and perfectly in my heart

I often wonder if I deserve such a prize
I often wonder if this prize will slip away
I often wonder at the wonder of having such a prize
as
steadfast friend, ally in all things,
gentle, positive analyst, loving wife

I know that the precious
must be appreciated and cared for
I know that the most precious
must be completely appreciated and loved
I know that I shall always
fully and completely appreciate
I know that I shall always
fully and completely love
this most precious, prized person

until my ability to appreciate
until my ability to love
Have withered and washed away

Simple Symbol

Once
A dream of complete love
boiled, roiled
In the troubled recess
of a sad, searching heart
Pleading for life

Then
Like a miracle
The dream took form, took substance
Became real, vital, living
Embodied, emboldened
in and around you

Now
Surrounding, engulfing, uplifting
The dream, no longer a dream
Brightens my darkness
Enhances my life
Extends my hope

To say thank you
To say how much I love you
I try to pick up
little gratitude pieces
Somehow missed in the onrush
of exhilarating change

This offering is one of these pieces
Missed but not forgotten
Simple symbol, circling, never ending
Testifying in small, yet significant way
To love that rings all reasons, all seasons

MORE BEAUTIFUL

Sweeter than honey
Softer than early morning dew

Warm like a soft, summer breeze
Hot and passionate like an inferno

Gentle
As easy falling mist

Caring
More than anyone can care

Loving more
More than anyone can love

Brilliant gem
Surrounding me in a rainbow of light

Growing younger with each joyful birthday
While growing more beautiful

Focus

I look out my study window
at the easy flow of Narragansett Bay
So reassuring in the steady pace
So seducing as it catches and
eagerly reflects the bright sunlight

Its tranquil countenance
intermittently dotted with bobbing boats
Seamlessly stitched with streaking wakes
Now witnessing and supporting a lumbering ship

Rolling south with subtle strength
and serene majesty
Still, I sense and worry about a shy sensitivity
To turmoil, to sudden storms, to thoughtlessness,
to not being appreciated

While I feast on its beauty
Marvel at its underlying power
Value its life sustaining, enhancing force
I wonder how I could protect it
from harm

In this time suspended state
I drift to thought of Annmarie
So like the Bay, in so many a way,
When I'm jolted into remembering
that today is her birthday

What to offer on this memorable day
Why not assurance against turmoil,
sudden storms and thoughtlessness

Why not appreciation springing freely
from complete love

The Bay will have to wait
wait until tomorrow for further
attention and related introspection
the sole focus this milestone day
will be my first, last and only true love

Annmarie

THIS WAY

I get out of bed
on one sturdy leg
It could be a different way
I look lovingly back to the person
who slept beside me. It could
be a different way. I eat milk-drenched, crunchy oats,
red strawberries. It could be a different way. I kiss,
wave goodbye, feel longing.
It could be a different way.
I read, write, take Sirius
to open fields. Doing what
I like. Feel longing. It could
be a different way. Later, eating dinner together, by
a fire, at a table with
softly burning, pink candles,
sweet music playing, longing
is washed away. It could
be a different way. Then
holding close, warm in a small
bed, in a big room, by another
fire. Longing not even a faint
whisper. It could be a different
way.
I want all days like this day.
No day ever to be a different
way.

Capturing Time

Birthdays expanding
Time diminishing

Our years slip quietly in
Then rush madly away

Slow their terrible pace
With firm and gentle reins

Lower the speed limits
Shut down the exits

Temper the rush to nowhere
Temper with light direction

Drink in the days
As they roll softly by

Sip the hours
Taste the sweetness

Make time the captive
Of our loving hands

Make time the captive
Of our loving hearts

The Waiting

I waited so long
for you to be born
to join with me, even
graduated high school
when you began life,
not knowing, yet dreaming
of dark beauty, bright love

I waited so long
while you played, stiffened with starch
longed, achieved, missed targets, languished

I was young, knowing, unknowing
busy seeking, languishing too,
while hitting baseballs, hiding defects,
sitting at desks, reading, scribbling,
this, that, still waiting

I became older, wary, whipped by emptiness,
hustled by fame, fortune, lashed by fate,
failure, talking myself hoarse in
a prison of solitude, learning to grieve,
grieve again, swaying in minds of
change, chance, grounded in
flavorless desperation, molded in despair
still waiting

Then our predestined souls finally reached,
finally touched, quickly followed by
powerfully invading love, which easily
routed tears, fears, mourning, with heat, with
brightness, healing hurts with balm,
bringing presence, spirit, meaning with hope
waiting no more

MYSTERY

Joining together
mercurial years ago
for a strange, unknown journey
going where, anywhere

An unlikely, likely pair
escaping from difference, diffidence, demand
weaving through hazard, hate, strife
suspecting, deep within, the value, the promise
taking intuitive, yet somewhat knowing, chance
leaving protection, safety, staidness behind
moving on, together, to shadowy adventure

Looking back at squandered funds, property, dreams
Looking now at the pull, push, necessary
stretch of meaningful living
Looking forward to open time, free, unhindered
Looking all times at ever growing, blooming love

Mysterious journey begun with a good companion
Easier journey continued with a better companion
Joyful journey ongoing forever with the
best of loving companions

ABOUT THE EDITOR

John McKenna Jr. is an actor, writer, director, musician and teacher. His published novels include *The Quiet Child* and *The Story Wizard*. His play *The Early Pre-Dusk of Doctor Menace's Re-Animated, Undead Zombies – or - Menace of the Morgue*, a musical zombedy, is being produced at The Casino Theater in Newport, Rhode Island, in October of 2011.